Equipping Christian Warriors for the Last Days

DR. DONALD BELL
MAJOR USMC RET.

Equipping Christian Warriors for the Last Days

October 2022
Copyright © Dr. Don Bell

All rights reserved. Printed in the United States of America. No part of this publication may be reproduced, stored in a retrieval system, or transmitted, in any form or by any means electronic, mechanical, photocopying, recording, or otherwise, without the prior written permission of the author.

Scripture taken from the Holy Bible, New International Version®, NIV®. Copyright © 1973, 1984, 201 Biblica, Inc.™ Used by permission of Zondervan. All rights reserved worldwide. www.zondervan.com The "NIV" and "New International Version" are trademarks registered in the United States Patent and Trademark Office by Biblica, Inc.™ All rights reserved.

Scripture quotations are from the Holy Bible, English Standard Version® (ESV®), copyright © 2001 by Crossway, a publishing ministry of Good Publishers. Used by permission. All rights reserved.

Scripture quotations taken from the New American Standard Bible®, Copyright © 1960, 1962, 1963, 1968, 1971, 1972, 1975, 1977, 1995 by Lockman Foundation, Used by permission. (www.lockman.org)

Because of the dynamic nature of the Internet, any web address or links contained in this book may have changed since publication and my no longer be valid. The views expressed in this work are solely those of the author and do not necessarily reflect the views of the publisher, and the publisher hereby disclaims any responsibility for them.

ISBN 978-1-943412-43-3

Published by -
Wilderness Voice Publishing, LLC
Canon City, Colorado USA
www.mcgmin.com

"A voice crying in the wilderness - proclaiming the good news of the coming Kingdom!"

CONTENTS

Mission Objective	4
Developing Our Mission In The Army Of God	5
Warrior-Spirited Christians Discern the Times	6
Coming to America	8
World Governments will soon War against the True Church	9
Ordeals Experienced By Leaders In The Army Of God	10
Christian Warriors – Enduring Persecution	12
Evil Disguised As Decency	13
Handling Suffering In The Army Of God	13
Overcoming "FEAR"	14
Our Lord Tarries	15
Walking As God's Warriors Day To Day	15
A Pure Church will Arise	16
Anointed Christian Warriors & the Final Gospel Proclamation	16
A Time of Great Harvest	17
The Army of God is for "VOLUNTEERS" Only	17
Leadership Priorities in the Kingdom of God	18

Equipping Christian Warriors for the Last Days

Mission Objective –

Calling for Warrior-Spirited Christians to network with one-another to stand and confront the challenges that await our generation.

My dear warrior-spirited Christian friends,

We are right on the verge of devastating events that will create great fear and chaos throughout the world and primarily, in the "Divided States of America."

- Today, so many Americans are aware that world events have been rapidly accelerating downhill toward a time of nation-wide disasters that our country has never before experienced.
- There is no doubt among many discerning American Christians that our once proud and mighty nation is shortly heading for a great and terrible fall. For Jesus warned us that "a nation divided against itself cannot stand." And I personally believe that this hate-filled division is so great, that America will never again be a united nation.

However, committed Christians who truly believe that our Lord is in control of these coming events need not be kept in the dark concerning the times that lie before us.

- For The Lord Jesus Christ, our true Commander-in-Chief in the Army of God has already provided detailed intelligence concerning those events which will precede His return to set up the Kingdom of God throughout the entire earth.
- This intelligence has been primarily recorded in the Book of Revelation which is a writing that has confused many in the church over the centuries. Yet, our Lord promises great blessings to those who read, hear and keep the prophetic messages communicated in the Book of Revelation.
- Listen to His words at both at the beginning and at the end of this Book:

> **_Blessed_** *is the one who reads aloud the words of this prophecy, and **_blessed_** are those who hear, and who keep what is written in it, for the time is near.* **Revelation 1:3**

> *"And behold, I am coming soon.* **_Blessed_** *is the one who keeps the words of the prophecy of this book."* **Revelation 22:7**

Certainly, the Book of Revelation has been a blessing to those truly committed churches through the centuries. It provided encouragement for many Christians concerning God's purposes in the midst of challenging times leading to persecution and martyrdom. This resulted in an uncompromising faith as they continued to look forward to the time of the New Heavens & Earth where they would abide forever with their Lord.

But also, since the Book of Revelation was written over 1900 years ago, millions of Christians over the centuries could not relate these prophetic events to their respective generations. Thus, the importance of the Book of Revelation has been pretty much ignored or downplayed by developing non-offensive theologies that would not scare or offend their respective churches.

However, we cannot continue to ignore or downplay these prophetic events any longer for they are soon coming. I truly believe that we are currently at a point in biblical history where many of these mysteriously challenging events recorded in the Book of Revelation will actually take place within our current generation. These are events which will precede the coming of our Lord Jesus to setup His millennial kingdom on earth. Exciting, but also challenging for this generation of Christendom.

So why is the understanding of the Book of Revelation so important for Christians in our current generation?

Answer: The Book of Revelation together with other prophetic books is primarily intended to provide Warrior-Spirited Christians with:

1. **Understanding** – of our times & God's purposes for coming judgments.
2. **Direction** – for our ministerial calling in the midst of these judgments.
3. **Preparation** – to "be ready" both spiritually & physically.
4. **Encouragement** - to be a "glorious light" within our respective environments during these challenging events which lie shortly before us.

Developing Our Mission In The Army Of God

The church in America is about to enter a very challenging time, which will open the doors in our nation for entry into its most fruitful times. The Darkness is gathering its forces, but so is the Light. The Lord has given each of us a specific part to play in His overall plan and it must be our continual quest to search for our individual mission assignment.

As we continue to move through the wilderness of this life, it is important for every Christian who has enlisted in the Army of God to know the mission that Jesus Christ has called them to, where they are at the present time, and the next step along the way. Almost everyone has a vision for what they want to accomplish, but it's going to require a difficult and continuous work discipline.

Every Christian that I have known has a desire to hear our Lord Jesus say, on that day when we enter into His presence:

> 'Well done, good and faithful servant. You have been faithful over a little; I will set you over much. Enter into the joy of your master. **Matthew 25:21**

Yet, not every Christian that enters into His presence will hear those words. Now, I'm not talking about salvation, but fulfilling our calling in this life which will lead to eternal rewards on the coming New Earth.

Each of us has an assigned mission that we must pursue and in order to hear those words we must move forward in the Lord and His mission for us. This doesn't mean simply being faithful in church attendance and tithing. That is all well and good but each of us has our own mission.

- Wherever you work, you have a mission – seek for it!
- Wherever you live, you have a mission – seek for it!

We are all called to be partakers of the work that God intends to complete which will usher in the reign of our Lord on this earth. If you don't complete your assigned mission, someone else will and then they will reap that reward that was initially set aside for you. *(Matthew 25:14-30)*

Consider this:

Many may have been called to enlist in the Army of God, yet they did not forsake their lives and thus did not achieve their full calling. They certainly are among the saints of God, but they did not attain to the leadership role that God had prepared them for. *(Luke 9:57-62)*

Every one of us faces these temptations toward apathy, as it is an ongoing attack from the enemy. Today, we must continually resist and prepare, for the Day of the Lord lies shortly before us.

Christian Warriors in the Army of God in these last days must be totally committed to walk the pathway that the Lord Jesus Christ, our true Commander-in-Chief, has laid before them. Therefore, it is important to internalize our understanding of the mission to which He has called us. This mission exists in the passion of each Christian's heart and direction becomes clearer as it is written down, prayed over, and internalized each day.

WARRIOR-SPIRITED CHRISTIANS DISCERN THE TIMES

This is not the time for God's people to withdraw into passivity and refuse to look at the reality of a rapidly decaying society that affects all of us and our loved ones.

We are not free to play the role of civilians, living as if there was no war. Our military role in the Army of God is pictured for us throughout the Bible; for the history of the saints in every age is one of conflict.

Therefore, we must have a deeper understanding of the spiritual warfare in light of our 21st century technology if we are to properly prepare for His coming; for we have been commanded to stay ready and alert by our true Commander-in-Chief Himself, our Lord Jesus Christ.

Listen to Jesus scolding those who fail to discern the times:

> **Interpreting the Time**
> *He also said to the crowds, "When you see a cloud rising in the west, you say at once, 'A shower is coming.' And so it happens. And when you see the south wind blowing, you say, 'There will be scorching heat,' and it happens.*
> *You hypocrites! You know how to interpret the appearance of earth and sky, but why do you not know how to interpret the present time?* **Luke 12:54-56**

Now, the prophet Daniel, who saw similar events over 2,500 years ago that would confront a future, end-time generation, was told by the Angel of the Lord when these events would take place:

> **The Time of the End**
> *And those who are wise shall shine like the brightness of the sky above; and those who turn many to righteousness, like the stars forever and ever. But you, Daniel, shut up the words and seal the book, until the time of the end.*
> - ***Many shall run to & fro, and knowledge shall increase." Daniel 12:3-4***

I submit to you that in our generation, technology has developed to a degree that allows us to relate such visions that both John and Daniel saw and recorded many centuries ago to our 21st century culture. For example:

"Many shall run to & fro"
- **"Many"** – The world now has a population of approximately 8 billion peoples.
- **"Run To & Fro"** - Airplanes, trains, automobiles, etc allow people to easily travel from country to country as well as daily visit shopping malls and movies that may be miles away.

"Knowledge shall increase" = consider the technology of today:
- **Television, cell phones, and internet** - Allows people to witness and participate in daily activities throughout the world.
- **Telecommunications** – Allows people to communicate with anyone, anytime, anywhere in the world.
- **Weaponry** – Today's nuclear technology endangers the great majority of the world's population.

Additionally, Daniel was told who would understand the times and who would not:

> *The Angel of the Lord said, "Go your way, Daniel, for the words are shut up and sealed until the time of the end. Many shall purify themselves and make themselves white and be refined, but the wicked shall act wickedly.*
> - ***And none of the wicked shall understand, but those who are wise shall understand.***
> ***Daniel 12:9-10***

Now, when will the Lord return?

No One Knows That Day and Hour

> *"But concerning that day and hour no one knows, not even the angels of heaven, nor the Son, but the Father only.* **Matthew 24:36**

However, Jesus does provide some clues concerning the season of His coming.

Jesus provides insight into the time of the end:

> *...For there will be great distress upon the earth and wrath against this people. They will fall by the edge of the sword and be led captive among all nations, and Jerusalem will be trampled underfoot by the Gentiles, until the times of the Gentiles are fulfilled.*
> **Luke 21:23-24**

The time of the Gentiles is that period of time when the holy city of Jerusalem is under the dominion of Gentiles (non-Jewish people).

- It was 70AD when the Romans warred against the Jews and destroyed the holy temple. Then in 135AD, following another Jewish rebellion, the Romans dispersed the Jewish people from the land of Israel.

The city of Jerusalem was then under the control of a multitude of Gentile nations for over 1800 years. Finally, in 1967 following the six day war, the Jews once again took control of the West Bank and the city of Jerusalem.

- **Thus, the time of the Gentiles ended in June, 1967.**

The Lesson of the Fig Tree

Jesus used the "fig tree" parable when teaching His disciples concerning the last days:

> *"From the fig tree learn its lesson: as soon as its branch becomes tender and puts out its leaves, you know that summer is near. So also, when you see all these things, you know that he is near, at the very gates. Truly, I say to you, this generation will not pass away until all these things take place.* **Matthew 24:32-34**

It is commonly understood by many theologians that the usage of "fig tree" in Scripture is frequently representative of the nation of Israel.

- Now, the coming forth of the leaves is prophetically accepted by many to be the establishment of Israel as a nation on May 14, 1948.
- If that is correct, then our generation will not pass away until all these things take place. "All these things" include His 2nd coming to establish the millennial kingdom on earth.

Additionally, we can literally see the numerous warning signs contained in Matthew 24 as well as Romans 1 unfolding before our very eyes today. These are signs which are the beginning of birth pains of the Great Tribulation. For example:

- Ethnic groups will arise against ethnic groups – hatred is intensifying among different racial groups and today's liberal hatred toward conservative Americans is horrific.
- Wars and rumors of wars – I personally believe that our world is soon heading to a World War that will destroy 1/3 of the earth and its populations (Revelation 8 & 9)

An Interesting Insight

One of our very early church fathers by the name of Polycarp, was a disciple and also a close friend of the Apostle John. Obviously Polycarp would have received tremendous insights from the man who experienced and recorded the Book of Revelation. Now, Polycarp was later martyred, but before his death, he also taught others concerning the end of times. One of his well-known disciples was Irenaeus who wrote a book called "Against Heresies."

In this book, Irenaeus says the following:

> "As God views 1,000 years as a day and He created the earth in 6 days and rested on the 7th, so shall the earth last for 6,000 years and rest under the reign of Christ for the last 1,000 years."

Here was a man who was taught by a friend of John's stating that Jesus Christ would return to reign on earth for one-thousand years which would represent a period of rest from six-thousand years of sinful, rebellious living in the world.

- Also, we should take note that the timeframe revealed in the Bible puts us very close to the completion of six-thousand years since the time of creation as recorded in the Bible.

These are end-times events which are quite mystifying for the great majority of God's chosen ones - but it is extremely critical for our generation of Christians who will be among the **"wise servants"** who discern the times and who are called to **"be ready."**

> *Therefore you also must **be ready**, for the Son of Man is coming at an hour you do not expect.*
> - *"Who then is the faithful and **wise servant**, whom his master has set over his household, to give them their food at the proper time?*
> - *Blessed is that **servant** whom his master will find so doing when he comes.*
> - *Truly, I say to you, he will set him over all his possessions.*   **Matthew 24:44-47**

In Summary:

1. Daniel was told that the time of the end would occur when "many shall run to and fro; and knowledge would increase." (Obviously, our generation can relate to this)
2. The time of the Gentiles ended in 1967 following the 6 day war.
3. The fig tree began producing fruit in 1948 and it was told that the time of the end would take place within the generation that was born within that time. That is – today's generation.
4. The warning signs in Matthew 24 and Romans 1 are unfolding before the eyes of those who truly have spiritual discernment of the times.
5. Irenaeus's prediction of the time of the millennial kingdom would occur 6,000 years from the beginning of the creation of mankind

COMING TO AMERICA

The United States as a democratic nation is rapidly disappearing – constitutional law will soon be ignored. As Christians, we cannot put our trust in financial institutions or government promises. All this is of the world and God's people need to come out of the world.

Those of us who correctly discern the times recognize that God's righteous judgment will soon descend upon America.

What type of Judgment?

- There have been numerous times in the history of the world when our Lord rained down judgments from heaven. Such as: earthquakes, plagues, hurricanes, tornados, etc.
- However, throughout history our Lord has also chosen to stir up the hearts of nations ruled by evil governments to launch attacks upon a nation that has historically known and worshipped Him, but have fallen into immorality and left Him to pursue their own sinful desires.

Think about these scenarios:

- A sudden economic collapse much like the 1929 stock market crash that occurred overnight resulting in sudden bank closures, multiple suicides, famine, diseases, families being thrown out of their homes. All this launched the great depression of the 1930's.

- Multiple nuclear terrorist strikes that will suddenly hit many cities (probably coastal) in our nation and before ordinary folks like us can adjust; the grocery stores, banks, and gas stations will be locked down. Because of our government's "open border" policy, I do believe that it is very possible that terrorists of today are smuggling in suitcase nukes to various cities and waiting for orders to launch coordinated nuclear attacks across our once beloved nation.
- Consider what American life would look like a few seconds after and EMP (electromagnetic pulse) incident - a nuclear weapon detonated high above the center of the United States. This would result in a large number of automobiles, airplanes, computers, cellular networks, home electricity, etc throughout our nation being immediately rendered useless. Over the past few years, barely a month goes by when some scientific organization or military expert warns that this scenario is very realistic.
- Whatever the scenario, it will certainly be a series of "sudden" catastrophic events unforeseen by the great majority in this country. These event(s) will surely launch more devastation than thousands of 9-11 disasters.

Resulting in:

- Great panic as people swarm to the banks, the grocery stores, the gas stations. They will not have a "customer mentality" – but a panicky, uncontrollable mob with no direction other than to grab and run with no concern with who gets hurt.

Immediate after-effects:

- Neighbors beating on neighbors doors seeking food. Stone throwing – breaking windows. Caring not for who gets hurt.
- Subsequently, after scourging the urban areas, youth gangs will form and go out to the suburban areas. Their intent is to intimidate families, burglarize homes, and murder those who oppose them.
- These "mob-gangs" will eventually organize with one another to kill and rob for food and other products which will become very valuable in a famine-plagued nation.

Governmental Response:

- Government militia forces will eventually unite to bring their version of "order" to the urban areas. History tells us that militia forces will attempt to confiscate all firearms as well as the storage of foods and supplies.

I am not trying to be pessimistic; this is a reality that lies before us and I want to alert my family and friends to "prepare now." The ones who are "prepared" are more ready to confront their fears in a period of sudden chaos.

This time of tremendous challenge is rapidly approaching and in the near future, we will need to stand "shoulder to shoulder" with one another and work together in developing our personal missions focusing upon how we will move forward from here.

And this is the purpose for forming a Watchmen Team on the Olympic Peninsula as well as others throughout our nation. That is:

- **Calling for Warrior-Spirited Christians to network with one-another to stand and confront the challenges that await our generation.**

World Governments will soon War against the True Church

Following the soon coming devastations that will remove our nation as the top-ranking economic power in the world, America will visibly unite with other nations and develop a list of those they believe to be the greatest threat to the plans for a worldwide "Great Reset."

- This "Great Reset" is really the deep state Globalists taking over the world and YOU!
- The mongrels of this "Great Reset" are the Giants of technology, business, international bankers, and global organizations like the UN, WHO, Gates Foundation, royal house of Britain, leftist politicians, etc.

And guess who will be seen as the greatest threat to the Deep State plans for a "Great Reset" that is designed to control the population of the entire world?

- Answer: They are the warrior-spirited Christians who proclaim that a "Divine Reset" is soon coming to destroy the "Great Reset" when the Lord Jesus Christ returns once again to establish the Kingdom of God throughout the entire earth.
- These are Christian-warriors who refuse to submit to the wicked authority of this world government and maintain that it is Jesus Christ who is their King. They will be deeply hated and the world will continually wage war against them.
- Thus, if American cities are struck by terrorists, we Christians may be the first to be blamed and labeled as the greatest enemy to national security. Even if Muslim terrorists are behind these terrorist attacks, Christians may still be blamed for being the major cause of Islamic hatred toward Americans.

History tells us that:

- All Bibles and Biblically related books will be outlawed except for government-supporting leadership in compromising churches. The peoples will be required to turn them over to the authorities for burning. Those who refuse will be criminally charged and sentenced to imprisonment.
- Torture, executions, imprisonment in concentration camps, separation from family, and forbidding the purchase of food and water will all be commonly employed tactics of this evil kingdom.
- These will be extremely hard and faith-challenging days and a time of "wearing out" the people of God, but Warrior-Spirited Christians in the Army of the Lord will remain steadfast throughout this brief period of time.

Do YOU Want To Be Among These Warrior-Spirited Christians?

Ordeals Experienced By Leaders In The Army Of God

God's leaders of this generation must understand, and internalize the following truths if they intend to prevail in their spiritual assignments:

- The great warriors of the Bible always went through periods of darkness before they were brought into the purposes of God.
- Between those places where we receive the promise and the fulfillment of the promise, there will be a challenging wilderness experience that few Christians understand when it rises up before them.
- The purpose of our wilderness journey is to conform us into the image of Jesus Christ and to bring us to a place of maturity where He can trust us with more authority.
- Many Christians will never walk in the promises of God to which they were called because, like the ancient Israelites, they will fall into whining, grumbling, and complaining about their wilderness experiences.
- Remember warriors, there is no victory without a battle. We must see every test as a great opportunity and no matter how dark it seems to get, the light will surely dawn, just as the sun comes up in the morning.

Some Biblical examples of Warriors standing for the Kingdom of God:

God's Warrior(s)	versus	Satan's Worldly Warrior(s)
David	versus	Goliath
Moses	versus	Pharaoh
Jacob	verses	Esau, his brother & Laban, his uncle
Joseph	verses	His 10 brothers & Pontiphar's wife
Moses, Joshua & Caleb	verses	Two-million whining Israelites
Gideon & 300 Men	verses	Army of 15,000 Midianites
Elijah on Mount Carmel	versus	Ahab, Jezebel, & 450 Prophets of Baal
Esther & Mordecai	verses	Haman & his plot to kill all Jews
Christian Martyrs	verses	Holy Roman Empire & Bloody Monarchs

21st Century

Christian Warriors	verses	World Governments & False Religions

For 6,000 years:

Kingdom of God	verses	Kingdom of World

Note, these men did not start out in church leadership positions – they received leadership anointing as they continually sought the Lord's direction for their lives.

These events certainly stand out, but we need to remember that the whole history of the church is a battlefield where God's people are confronted again and again by Satan's chosen vessels.

Satan's worldly warriors, who are supported by dark governments and pagan religions, will always visibly appear to be greater and more powerful than God's warriors.

- Yet, warrior-spirited Christians standing uncompromisingly for our Lord will always prevail in the strength of the Lord.
- The praying believer will never faint during hard times. On the contrary, he will grow stronger and stronger – because he trusts in God before he trusts in men.

> *He gives power to the faint, and to him who has no might he increases strength. Even youths shall faint and be weary, and young men shall fall exhausted; but they who **wait** for the Lord shall renew their strength; they shall mount up with wings like eagles; they shall run and not be weary; they shall walk and not faint.* **Isaiah 40:29-31**

Christian warriors need to remember that this is a Holy War and that the required power for victory is not found among its human participants, but in the power of God.

- Thus, believers need to understand the power of prayer which may be likened to that wrestling which took place between God and his chosen warriors throughout history.
- This is the "ongoing battle" that should be taking place within each member of the Body of Christ.

Believers must prevail with God before Satan can be subdued in their lives.

- Believers will never prevail by battling in the flesh. The victory is to be the Lord's and Christians can only prevail if they humble themselves before Him in true heart repentance.
- Prayerlessness is proof that our life is still under the power of the flesh. It proves that the life of God in the soul is mortally sick and weak. Prayerlessness is the cause of a powerless spiritual life.

Victory is certain if believers will exercise the patient, long-suffering faith that brought His mighty warriors through the battlefield.

As Christians, we have been brought into the story of life at this time in the history of the world in order to enlist in the Army of God.

- Believers need to put on the armor of God and allow His Light to shine through them in the workplace, their neighborhoods, and their families. These places are the true front lines of the battlefield.

> *"You are the light of the world. A city set on a hill cannot be hidden. Nor do people light a lamp and put it under a basket, but on a stand, and it gives light to all in the house. In the same way, let your light shine before others, so that they may see your good works and give glory to your Father who is in heaven."* **Matthew 5:14-16**

Remember, all of God's biblical warriors did lose some battles now and then, but they continued to be strengthened by their experiences and did not succumb to self-pity.

- That warrior spirit may be knocked down on occasion but will always seek the strength of the Lord in order to get back up and again run to the battle. **These are the Christian warriors who will "never quit."**

Christian Warriors – Enduring Persecution

My brothers & sisters in Christ, the time may soon come when He calls us to the following:

> *If anyone is to be taken captive, to captivity he goes; if anyone is to be slain with the sword, with the sword must he be slain. Here is a call for the endurance and faith of the saints.* **Rev. 13:10**

In the coming days, true believers in Jesus Christ will be challenged from every direction. Every believer who commits to an all-out relationship with our Lord will come under governmental oppression, various afflictions, and persecution.

- We may initially struggle in our trials because discipline and suffering is foreign to us, but as we continue to endure – our hearts will continually grow deeper in our love and commitment to Him.
- At times it may seem unbearable when some friends and even family members become spiteful toward us. Yet, enduring the scorn and persecution from the world joins us in a partnership with Christ as we share in His sufferings in this life.

We need to be mindful that being persecuted is a blessed opportunity to honor Christ?

> *"Blessed are you when others revile you and persecute you and utter all kinds of evil against you falsely on my account. Rejoice and be glad, for your reward is great in heaven, for so they persecuted the prophets who were before you.* **Matthew 5:11-12**

Suffering with Christ produces a strong heart bond in our relationship with Him and with one another as we follow Him down the same path that He walked.

Listen to Paul speaking to his disciple, Timothy:

> *Share in suffering as a good soldier of Christ Jesus. No soldier gets entangled in civilian pursuits, since his aim is to please the one who enlisted him.* **2 Timothy 2:3-4**

An awareness of one of God's purposes for tribulation should also strengthen us during these times:

> *For when your judgments are in the earth, the inhabitants of the world learn righteousness.* **Isaiah 26:9**

Also, remember that our Lord's mighty hand will be upon us during these times, and nothing can touch us without His authorization:

> *He will cover you with his pinions, and under his wings you will find refuge; his faithfulness is a shield and buckler. You will not fear the terror of the night, nor the arrow that flies by day, nor the pestilence that stalks in darkness, nor the destruction that wastes at noonday. A thousand may fall at your side, ten thousand at your right hand, but it will not come near you.* **Psalm 91:4-7**
> <u>***Also, remember David's faith when he said:***</u>
> *Even though I walk through the valley of the shadow of death, I will fear no evil, for you are with me; your rod and your staff, they comfort me.* **Psalm 23:4**

This is the time when we may be called to glorify our Lord by the laying down of our lives, but it will not happen until our mission in this life is complete.

Like the apostle Paul, some of us may also be called to witness with fellow prisoners in captivity.

- Those in prisons are more receptive to the Gospel since they have lost all hope in the world.
- Many that are in prison are truly "free" in the spirit while many outside the prison walls who are enjoying the riches received in this world are unknowingly "spiritual prisoners."

> <u>***Count it all joy***</u>, *my brothers, when you meet trials of various kinds, for you know that the testing of your faith produces steadfastness. And let steadfastness have its full effect, that you may be perfect and complete, lacking in nothing.* **James 1:2-4**

Evil Disguised As Decency

- Evil disguised as decency in the midst of a lukewarm Christian community, may be strong weapons the enemy will use against you. Even friends and family members will attack your faith and attempt to get you to make compromises so that life won't be so hard. **<u>Stand fast!</u>**
- During these times of persecution, the voice of Satan will undoubtedly attack many with, "this is too hard.... it's not fair.... God has forsaken me." Be aware that when these thoughts begin to surface that you are a soldier in the Army of God under attack. **<u>Stand fast!</u>**
- This will be tough when loved ones embrace you and try to get you to compromise your faith just a little bit by saying, "God will understand." **<u>Stand fast</u>**!
- Your steadfastness is of tremendous importance to both you and your loved ones who are considering small compromises. It will have a powerful strengthening effect on all who see your uncompromising testimony which prioritizes the Kingdom of God over the world.
- Your family and friends may grieve over your steadfastness that leads to persecution, but they too will be strengthened in their lives.

Handling Suffering In The Army Of God

The Lord's word tells us that suffering is a necessary experience that His warriors must endure in order to receive His glory. Being "prepared" doesn't mean we won't suffer.

> *The Spirit himself bears witness with our spirit that we are children of God, and if children, then heirs — heirs of God and fellow <u>heirs with Christ, provided we suffer with him</u> in order that we may also be glorified with him.* **Romans 8:16-17**

- This truth will be severely tested when the trumpets continue to blast forth devastation upon the earth for then; we will be expected to confront our personal sufferings in order that we will not be derailed from our calling during that critical time.

Suffering is a means by which God breaks the vessel so that His glory might be revealed, but only if we respond in the proper way. One might ask, "What actually is suffering?"

- Suffering may be physical, or it may be mental or emotional, but suffering really is anything that we don't like; anything that is uncomfortable or painful for us.
- Certainly, the most painful suffering that may occur would be the loss of our loved ones, but our heavenly Father understands this, for He also experienced the loss of His Son. Our hope in such a grievous situation derives from understanding that - as the Father raised His Son from the dead, that our loved ones who die in Christ will also be raised to eternal life with Him.

It is through suffering in life that warrior-spirited Christians develop the characteristics of holiness, that will allow them to become more and more conformed to the image of His Son.

- Characteristics such as a strong compassion for people, a spirit that is slow to anger, a passionate desire for truth and justice, and the ability to forgive our enemies; these all develop within as the Christian experiences personal suffering. A proper handling of life's sufferings will burn away inner pride and ego – it purifies His people, especially the one's chosen for leadership.
- Sufferings in life should no longer be a surprise, yet Christians must learn to handle them today so we will be prepared tomorrow, when the trumpets begin to blast.

> *... when you do good and **suffer** for it you endure, this is a gracious thing in the sight of God. For to this you have been called, because **Christ also suffered for you**, leaving you an example, so that you might follow in his steps.*
>
> *He committed no sin, neither was deceit found in his mouth. When he was reviled, he did not revile in return; **when he suffered**, he did not threaten, but continued entrusting himself to him who judges justly.*
>
> *He himself bore our sins in his body on the tree, that we might die to sin and live to righteousness. By his wounds you have been healed. **1 Peter 2:20-24***

We must stand as warriors in the midst of good times and bad times; for both will be faced in life.

OVERCOMING "FEAR"

Fear has the tendency to cause people to stick their heads in the sand and hope this won't happen. It will keep us from properly preparing and that day of tremendous warfare will then drop on us like a thief in the night.

Our generation is going to face some very challenging times and more and more Christian warriors are needed for a tough battlefield that will bring forth a great multitude of people that will give their lives over to the Lord –

- These are peoples who will be searching for men and women of great spiritual strength in the midst of tremendous tribulations - those who are **not fearful** during these times.

I have learned from my Vietnam War experiences that the key to overcoming fear in warfare is by prioritizing the men under your authority over your own life. For example:

- In the midst of a very fierce firefight I learned that when I prioritized the men under my authority ahead of my own life, the spirit of fear could not control my decisions.
  - Now think about your loved ones in the midst of times when needed supplies will no longer be available and it will free you to make appropriate decisions concerning preparations.
- This is not the time for God's people to withdraw into passivity – to refuse to look at the reality of **a rapidly decaying society** that affects all of us and our loved ones.

- We are not free to play the role of **civilians**, living as if there was no war. Our **military** role is pictured for us throughout the bible; for the history of the saints in every age is one of conflict.

Prioritize your family & friends before you and "fear" will no longer be in control of your decisions.

Our Lord Tarries

Day and night throughout the centuries, God's intercessors have cried out to the Lord that His kingdom will come, and righteous judgment will occur on the earth. Yet our Lord tarries.

- Though He is at work every moment of every day, it is not always as we wish or in ways that are visible to us. He is on the throne of justice; so we may wonder just how long justice can be postponed.
- Yet we must remember that He is also on the throne of grace. This grace is intended not only for those being persecuted but also for their persecutors.
- If postponement of justice for one more day results in bringing one more person into the Kingdom of God, then so be it. Remember, for the Lord a thousand years is like a single day.
- If a million years from now we were to ask ourselves whether our momentary suffering during our earthly life was an acceptable exchange for one more soul to enter into eternal glory, how would we answer?

When considering these hard, but wonderful truths, I am reminded of the Roman centurion who was in charge of the crucifixion of Christ.

Listen to him:

> *When the centurion and those who were with him, keeping watch over Jesus, saw the earthquake and what took place, they were filled with awe and said, "Truly this was the Son of God!" (Matthew 27:54)*

I wouldn't be surprised if this Roman centurion and some of his men, who led the military unit assigned to crucify our Lord, will reign with us in glory. In fact, historic tradition says that they did convert to Christianity.

- Such is the long-suffering of Him who sits on the throne of grace.

Walking As God's Warriors Day To Day

Redeeming the time may be extremely difficult, but it is also one of the most important areas of daily life that champion leaders must overcome.

- Stay on the offensive; take the Sword of the Spirit which is the Word of God and know it, memorize it, take it up daily.
- Anticipate the battle daily; allow it to cause a growth in strength and intimacy with the Lord.
- Stand firm, when under daily fire – remember the warriors of the bible. These are our brothers and sisters with whom we will one day reign in the eternal kingdom.

Intercessory prayer must become heart driven; for this is where your one on one relationship with the Lord truly grows powerful.

This is our call and for those who hear this call to be a warrior and overcomer; this is an opportunity that was offered to warriors like Paul, David, Elijah, etc; and it is offered to each of us in our life.

We only have one life and thus, one opportunity to stand for our Lord on the front lines of the battlefield and fight against His enemies.

- The rewards that are promised in the afterlife are predicated upon our kingdom work during this lifetime.
- Some will rule ten cities, some five, someone, but most will be citizens, not leaders.
- All will receive rewards, but there is a difference; His steadfast warriors will be called to leadership in the eternal kingdom.

Let us not go to the grave wishing that we had answered this call. Now is the time; not tomorrow or next week - the call is now to "those who hear".

Yes, Tremendous Tribulation Lies Before Us, But A Pure Church will Arise in the Midst of this Chaos

- A great apostasy will soon take place bringing a separation between light and darkness in the American churches.
- The "weeds" within the church will run but those who remain will truly represent the Kingdom of God to the many in our nation who are suffering great loss and grief.
- This will result in a pure testimony from the true church, causing many peoples to embrace the Lord Jesus during the times of tribulation which precede His 2nd coming to establish His eternal kingdom upon this earth.
- I truly foresee a great outpouring of the Holy Spirit upon this people like never before (even greater in numbers than the 1st century church). This will be the time that Jesus talked about when He said that **"greater works will you do than even I have done"**. He was speaking of national and worldwide messengers of God ministering in the great and glorious power of His Holy Spirit.
- **This is the Body of Christ that goes forth proclaiming the message of John the Baptist:**

> *"The voice of one crying in the wilderness: 'Prepare the way of the Lord; make his paths straight.'" Matthew 3:3*

- **But now it will be calling people to "prepare" for the 2nd coming of our Messiah, the Lord Jesus Christ.**

Anointed Christian Warriors & the Final Gospel Proclamation

Christian warriors of the end-time generation will boldly and fearlessly stand united against the apostasy of this age as they proclaim the testimony of Jesus Christ and His truths among all the nations of the earth.

> *And this gospel of the kingdom will be proclaimed throughout the whole world as a testimony to all nations, and then the end will come.* **Matthew 24:14**

As to the contents of their message during a time of tribulation, these anointed witnesses for Christ will continually stand before the Lord of the whole earth and they will speak nothing but that which their Lord has commissioned them to speak.

- They will speak of Christ and His atoning blood, which is the witness of the righteousness and holiness of God in the midst of a sinful world.

> *Jesus said to him, "I am the way, and the truth, and the life. No one comes to the Father except through me.* **John 14:6**
> *And there is salvation in no one else, for there is no other name under heaven given among men by which we must be saved."* **Acts 4:12**

- They will openly condemn all efforts to seek salvation outside of that atoning blood, and this will infuriate the false church as well as the worldly leadership that is attempting to establish a one-world kingdom.

A Time of Great Harvest

Yes, this will be a time of great tribulation never before seen since the creation of the earth, yet this also will be a time of a great harvest of souls.

- A time of tremendous miracles as the gospel message goes forth in a power greater than the world has ever seen: the blind will see, the deaf will hear, and many of the afflicted will be healed throughout the world.

> "Truly, truly, I say to you, whoever believes in me will also do the works that I do; and greater works than these will he do, because I am going to the Father. Whatever you ask in my name, this I will do, that the Father may be glorified in the Son. **John 14:12-13**

- The world must hear the Gospel message proclaimed by His end-time warrior-spirited witnesses and they must hear it repeatedly so that they become fully conscious of their sin and the redemptive work of Jesus Christ.
- All of mankind shall be well-acquainted with the Gospel message of Jesus Christ before the final judgments fall on the earth.
- And there will be no more grey areas; one stands either with Christ or against Him. Love and hatred will be clearly visible among all the inhabitants of the earth.
- Those who reject Him will do so willingly and deliberately. Then the testimony is finished and may be silenced.
- Those who scorn the message will be without excuse when they stand before the judgment seat of almighty God.
- Certainly many people will respond and be brought into everlasting life, but the great majority of the world will blaspheme this message and will persecute those who proclaim it.

Finally, this Gospel message not only will be a calling to mankind to repent and give glory to God, but it also will contain the prophetic warning that final judgments are soon coming to the world.

- Judgments that will usher in the coming of the King of Kings to setup the Kingdom of God upon the earth.
- This is in answer to millions of prayers that called to our Almighty God that "His Kingdom come and His will be done upon this earth, just as it is in heaven!" Amen!

The Army of God is for "VOLUNTEERS" Only

Obviously, my approach to addressing these end-time events is from a military perspective since much of who I am today is the result of my 20 years in the Marine Corps.

- The common purpose for all volunteers in the Army of God is to **prepare in the bootcamp of our prayer closets** in order to allow the light and glory of our Commander-in-Chief, Jesus Christ to be clearly manifested on the spiritual battlefield which lies in the midst of this world.
- Our Commander-in-Chief does not draft His soldiers, but He opens His arms and welcomes all those who volunteer. He does not employ emotional strategies, but simply speaks out of love and calls each of us to join Him on the battlefield.
- Although he calls us to join Him in His battle against the forces of evil, He leaves us free to join the enemy against Him if we so will. He makes no promises that we will become rich nor experience pain in this life.
- Christian warriors who will stand fast in teaching others and will not compromise the true gospel are His disciples whom He values deeply.

Our Choice – Will We or Won't We?

We are faced with the option of greatness as a leader in the Kingdom of God, but we can choose to settle for less. If we decide for greatness, it will cost us everything we have and are. We will have to surrender our life. The choice is momentous, but amazingly, it is ours to make.

Leadership Priorities in the Kingdom of God

- **1st** – We fight for the glory of His wondrous Name in the midst of a world of darkness.
- **2nd** – We fight for the salvation of those in bondage to the enemy. Family, friends, co-workers and strangers that our Lord brings into our lives.
- **3rd** – We fight without fear for ourselves for we are called to let go of this life and not be concerned for the consequences that may befall us.

Finally, my dear brothers and sisters who are hearing this message – may our Lord powerfully anoint you to be mighty warrior-spirited witnesses for the Lord Jesus Christ and the Kingdom of God as you travel though the wilderness of this life

> *Arise, shine, for your light has come, and the glory of the Lord has risen upon you. For behold, darkness shall cover the earth, and thick darkness the peoples; but the Lord will arise upon you, and his glory will be seen upon you.* **Isaiah 60:1-2**

Amen.

www.ingramcontent.com/pod-product-compliance
Lightning Source LLC
Chambersburg PA
CBHW081456060426

42444CB00037BA/3375